The
Rosary Project

29 August 2023

Peter N. Huyck

Editing, design and production
by M. H. Mulka

Cover photo by Artem Saranin

Independently published.
ISBN: 9798448615696

The
Rosary Project

by Peter Huyck

For Dominicus Prutenus

and the anonymous artist
who first carved the 15 mysteries
into woodblocks
at Ulm in 1483 AD

"The rosary is an excellent prayer,
but the faithful should feel serenely free
in its regard."

Pope St. Paul VI
Marialis Cultus

Contents

Preface..11

The Essential Rosary..............................15

Psalms for Each Decade Bead...................19

Original 14th & 15th Mysteries..................35

The Nonessential Additions......................39

      The Hail Mary........................40

      The Four Extra Beads...............43

      The Decade Beads...................45

      Other Additions......................46

Making a 55-Bead Rosary.........................48

Bibliography...50

Preface

The purpose of this brief treatise is to rediscover the rosary of 600 years ago—a version that I personally believe is both the purest and the best. To arrive at this point, though, we first must travel back to the beginning.

The history of prayer beads begins with followers of the Jain Dharma in India around 900 B.C. What sacred formulas they said to accompany their beads, unfortunately, is lost to time. What was not lost, though, was the practice of repetitious prayer.

The Jain custom of prayer beads spread to the Hindu sects and into Buddhism.

It crossed into Christianity in Egypt around 350 A.D., where there was contact with the East along the trade routes. One form it took among the Desert Fathers in Egypt was the Jesus Prayer ("Lord Jesus Christ, Son of God, have mercy on me a sinner" said on a string of 100 beads), which then spread into Greece and Russia.

A related form of prayer resulted from the migration of some of the Desert Fathers from Egypt to the islands off Ireland in the Dark Ages. There the lay brothers in the monasteries recited 150 Our Fathers on knotted cords (150 is the number of the Psalms).

This custom of saying 150 Our Fathers spread to the laity on the European continent sometime around the 10th century.

Beads replaced knotted cords among the common people. The Prayer of the Annunciation soon replaced the Our Father, perhaps because of a Marian revival at the time, or perhaps because it was shorter.

Meditations were first introduced for the beads in early 15th century Germany by a Carthusian monk named Dominicus Prutenus. Originally there was one thought for each of 50 beads in Dominicus' meditation. These 50 meditations for 50 beads evolved over the century to become 15 meditations for 150 beads. The prayer took off when a rough woodcut picture version of the 15 meditations appeared in a printed book at Ulm in 1483.

These images were immediately copied by other artists all over Europe. It is this rosary, with its 150 Annunciation prayers joined to 15 illustrated mysteries, that I, after decades of research and prayer, consider to be the rosary in its purest form.

But what happened? Why aren't we today praying this easy, repetitive prayer that can so simply help us tap into our connection with the divine?

Indeed, if you pick up a contemporary book on the rosary, its essence is barely discernible. (See, for example, the standard *Pray the Rosary* from the Catholic Book Publishing Corporation, which now runs at a whopping 112 pages.) However, if all the extra material is stripped away, the original rosary shines through, joining the Jesus Prayer, its cousin from the Egyptian desert, and the ancient prayer of the Jains, as a powerful psychophysical spiritual technique.

The version of the rosary presented here is meant to connect to this ancient prayer energy and return the rosary to its position as a gateway to contemplation.

— PH

The Essential Rosary

The essence of the rosary is to repeat, out loud or in your mind, 150 times, the words of Gabriel and Elizabeth, while counting the repetitions on beads and holding lightly in mind 15 set episodes from the Jesus story in succession throughout.

These are the words of Gabriel, according to Luke:

Hail, full of grace, the Lord is with you.

These are the words of Elizabeth to Mary, inspired by the Holy Spirit, again according to Luke:

Blessed are you among women,
and blessed is the fruit of your womb.

Elizabeth is reviewing for Mary what the angel has previously told her, thus giving Mary a human confirmation of the prophecy. Gabriel had prophesied "You have found favor with God" and "You will conceive in your womb and bear a son. He will be great and be called Son of the Most High."

The words of Gabriel and Elizabeth appear over and over in The Little Office of the Blessed Virgin Mary, as the versicle and responsory, in the 10th century. Mary herself would have had occasion to remember these words, one conjectures, given the context in which she first heard them and considering how events subsequently played out.

These words together, then, comprise the prayer of the Annunciation and Visitation:

Hail, full of grace, the Lord is with you.
Blessed are you among women,
and blessed is the fruit of your womb.

The string of 150 beads required to count this prayer one per bead is unwieldy, so the custom was to use 50 beads and go around three times. Soon, larger beads were added every ten beads, but no prayers were said on these decade beads. They were just there to help with the counting and for decoration—the decade beads were sometimes quite fancy.

To pray this essential rosary, simply say 150 Annunciation prayers—and no other prayers— counting them on beads (on a 59 bead rosary, just

Rosaries of the 16th century with 55 beads.

skip over the first four beads) and bring to mind the 15 Mysteries indicated by the Psalm passages in succession on the decade beads (you will soon have these memorized). The Psalm passages provide a springboard for meditation and ring in each new mystery.

Note that those who first prayed in this manner could not read and so likely recalled woodcut images instead of Psalm phrases. Either way, it is the thought that counts.

The mysteries used herein are the ones in common use today. They differ from the originals of 1483 AD in Mysteries 14 & 15. Much ink has been spilled over the Assumption of Mary into heaven and the Crowning of Mary as Queen of Heaven. This need not concern us, as our interest is in devotion, not theology. If they don't work for you, use the original 14th and 15th meditations from 1483. The 14th was the Dormition — the old legend that the apostles reassembled at Mary's deathbed. The 15th was Christ Triumphant over the rainbow, a common trope in the Middle Ages.

Psalms

for Each Decade Bead

I. ANNUNCIATION

I rejoiced to do your will

as though all riches were mine.

Ps. 118:14

II. VISITATION

My heart is ready, O God,

my heart is ready.

Ps. 5-6:8

III. NATIVITY

You are my son.

Ps. 2:7

IV. PRESENTATION

You do not ask for holocaust and victim.

Instead, here am I.

Ps. 39:78

V. FINDING IN THE TEMPLE

I burn with zeal for your house.

Ps. 68:10

VI. AGONY IN THE GARDEN

Call on me in the day of distress.

Ps. 49:15

VII. SCOURGING

They ploughed my back like ploughmen,
drawing long furrows.

Ps. 128:3

VIII. CROWNING WITH THORNS

Now that I am in trouble they gather,

they gather and mock me.

Ps. 34:15

IX. CARRYING THE CROSS

They go out, they go out, full of tears,
carrying seed for the sowing.

Ps. 125:6

X. CRUCIFIXION

Oh God, they have set

your sanctuary on fire.

Ps. 73:7

XI. RESURRECTION

The foe is destroyed,

eternally ruined.

Ps. 9:7

XII. ASCENSION

O Gates, lift high your heads;
grow higher, ancient doors.
Let him enter, the king of glory.

Ps. 23:7

XIII. PENTECOST

He sends out his word to the earth, and swiftly runs his command.

Ps. 147:15

XIV. ASSUMPTION OF MARY INTO HEAVEN

Of you my heart has spoken:
"Seek his face."

Ps. 26:8

XV. CORONATION OF MARY

He fixes the number of the stars;

he calls each one by its name.

Ps. 146:4

The Original

14th & 15th Mysteries

XIV. DORMITION

Of you my heart has spoken:
"Seek his face."

Ps. 26:8

XV. TRIUMPH OF CHRIST IN GLORY

From the ivory palace

you are greeted with music.

Ps. 44:9

The Nonessential Additions

The Hail Mary

Of first importance to praying the essential rosary is to return the Hail Mary to its 10th century form, as explained on pages 15-16 herein. The common version of the Hail Mary is deconstructed back into this original version by omitting the words in **bold** type as follows:

> Hail **Mary**, full of grace, the Lord is with **thee**.
> Blessed art **thou** among women and blessed is the fruit
> of **thy** womb, **Jesus. Holy Mary, Mother of God,**
> **pray for us sinners now and at the hour of our**
> **death. Amen.**

Consider, please, the following justifications for these admittedly substantial revisions.

The Names of Jesus and Mary

The name of Mary was added to the prayer early on, by popular usage; the addition of the name of Jesus came later, also by popular usage. But the names do not appear in the gospel and they were never attached to the versicle and responsory in *The Little Office of the Virgin Mary*. Though the names do not interfere much with the flow of the prayer, it is more powerful without them—the actual words according to Luke.

Thee, Thou, Thy

Elizabethan pronouns are not magical incantations. They were meant to be meant, and those who first uttered them (the Elizabethans) meant them. Use today's ordinary English to truly mean what you say today.

Holy Mary, Mother of God,
pray for us sinners now
and at the hour of our death.

This postscript sounds like it was written by a committee, and indeed it was. It was added by the Council of Trent in response to the Protestant charge that the Hail Mary was not a real prayer. The Protestants apparently thought that you're not really praying if you're not asking for something.

To say it now, though, seems akin to arguing the politics of 1545 as if they were still relevant. Plus, it almost doubles the length of what is supposed to be a short, ejaculatory prayer—and it is not scriptural. It also introduces a lot of unnecessary theological baggage that can (and should) be left out of the rosary.

Amen

This means "so be it." Some versions of the rosary have 167+ "amens" salted throughout like little sub-mantras. Do we need it, though? Not really. Omitting it removes the sense of "finality" it brings, allowing us to remain in an uninterrupted state of prayer.

The Four Extra Beads

An essential rosary has 55 beads; most commercially available rosaries have 59 beads. The initial four beads are usually assigned to faith, hope, and charity, along with an extra Our Father thrown in for the heck of it.

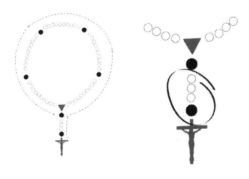

The 59-bead modern rosary with its four extra beads.

In fact, those initial four beads are a curious historical accident.

Three different prayers were said on the same set of 70 beads in 16th century England. All 70 were used for the Brigittine Rosary. The Crown of Thorns used only 33. The Marian rosary used only 55.

When the Brigittine Rosary and the Crown of Thorns fell out of favor, bead makers eliminated eleven beads but, for reasons unknown, failed to eliminate the other four. Aesthetics, perhaps?

They do look nice. Still, we can skip over them, remove them, or make a 55-bead rosary. Though we could all use more faith, hope and charity, we do not need an arbitrarily weighed-down rosary.

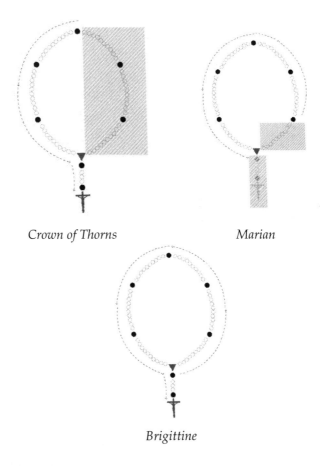

Crown of Thorns *Marian*

Brigittine

Rosaries of the 16th century.

The Decade Beads

The Our Father is Christianity's most cherished prayer and is, in fact, the prayer that was said on knotted cords in the Irish monasteries in the Dark Ages. But what is it doing here in our Marian rosary?

In the 14th century, someone began saying the Our Father on the previously naked decade beads, and it caught on. However, that in effect added speed bumps to the prayer cycle. Maintaining a rolling repetition instead will induce the deep contemplation we seek in prayer.

Other Additions

When we also eliminate the Intentions of the Pope, the Apostles Creed, the prayer for Faith, Hope and Charity, the Doxology, the virtue for each mystery, the fruits for each mystery, the Fatima Ejaculation, the mysteries of Light, the Hail, Holy Queen, and the Litany of Loretto, we are eliminating only the nonessential.

If we pray the 10th century version of the Hail Mary 150 times, and bring to mind the 15 mysteries on the decade beads, forsaking all other prayers, we soon find the doorway to wordless contemplation. This is the path laid out by the Jains and the Desert Fathers. By eliminating the nonessential, we have arrived at the essential.

The 55-bead essential rosary.

*"We live as though we were in Mary's rose garden,
those of us who occupy ourselves with the roses."*

~Dominicus Prutenus

Making a 55-Bead Rosary

Certainly the easiest way to return to the essential rosary is to use your current rosary and simply skip the four extra beads. However, much is to be said for returning your rosary to its earlier iteration with only 55 beads.

If you are fond of your current rosary and it is constructed of beads with metal pins, a pair of needle-nosed pliers will quickly remove the four extra beads.

Alternatively, you can make your own 55-bead rosary. I recommend 7mm-8mm gemstone, glass, or wooden beads strung with metal pins or twine. Plastic does not seem to carry the weight of the prayer, either literally or metaphysically. Following are three companies which handle the materials necessary for constructing a 55-bead rosary. All offer instructions for making a rosary, as well as the tools required.

Fire Mountain Gems and Beads	firemountaingems.com 800-355-2137
Lewis and Company	rosaryparts.com 800-342-2400
Our Lady's Rosary Makers	rosarymakingparts.com 502-936-1477

Bibliography

Huyck, Peter. *Rosary Psalms*, London: St. Pauls (UK), 1994.

Thurston, Fr. Herbert. *The Month*, (96{1900}: 403-18, 513-27, 627-37; 97{1901}: 67-79, 172-88, 286-304).

Winston-Allen, Anne. *Stories of the Rose: The Making of the Rosary in the Middle Ages*, University Park: University of Pennsylvania Press, 1997.

About the Author

Peter Huyck is the author of Scriptural Meditations for the Rosary (Mystic, Connecticut: Twenty-Third Publications, 1982), Rosary Psalms (St. Paul's, United Kingdom, 1994), and A Scriptural Rosary — 1596 (St. Paul's, United Kingdom, 1999). He lives in Iowa City, Iowa.

Made in the USA
Middletown, DE
05 August 2022